The Speckled People

Hugo Hamilton grew up in Dublin with an Irish father from West Cork and a German mother from the Rhineland who came to Ireland shortly after the Second World War. He is an acclaimed novelist and his best-selling memoir *The Speckled People* (2003) has found resonance right across the world. He lives in Dublin.

Hugo Hamilton

The Speckled People

Methuen Drama

Published by Methuen Drama 2011

Methuen Drama, an imprint of Bloomsbury Publishing Plc

1 3 5 7 9 10 8 6 4 2

Methuen Drama
Bloomsbury Publishing Plc
50 Bedford Square
London WC1B 3DP
www.methuendrama.com

Adapted by Hugo Hamilton from his memoir *The Speckled People*, published in
2003 by Fourth Estate, an imprint of HarperCollins*Publishers*

Play text copyright © Hugo Hamilton 2011

Hugo Hamilton has asserted his rights under the Copyright, Designs and Patents
Act 1988 to be identified as the author of this work.

ISBN 978 1 408 17118 9

A CIP catalogue record for this book is available from the British Library

Available in the USA from Bloomsbury Academic & Professional, 175 Fifth
Avenue/3rd Floor, New York, NY 10010. www.BloomsburyAcademicUSA.com

Typeset by Mark Heslington Ltd, Scarborough, North Yorkshire

The Speckled People

Author's Note: The Memory Room

Your childhood keeps coming after you, like your own name. One of the most frequent questions I have been asked since *The Speckled People* was first published in 2003 is how long it took to write this memoir. There is no straightforward answer to that question. It takes time to step back into your childhood, to dig through the rubble of memory, to find out what questions to ask about the past. It takes time to persuade yourself to open the hall door and let everyone in off the street to look around your family secrets. It takes time to unlock the silence cast over the family and to rescue flashes of half-suppressed memory into the safety of a story. It takes time to learn how to speak.

This was a story of confusion and regret and comical misunderstanding, a story of language conflict, and history bullying its way into the present around the breakfast table. We spoke German and Irish at home and walking out the front door on to the street was like a daily migration into the English language. Adapting the memoir to the stage for the Gate Theatre is not so much a retelling but a completely new way of explaining that childhood chaos. The language of the theatre reveals many things that I have not been aware of. The stage has become the memory room. So it could be said that my childhood is not only coming after me but also brought to life before me.

It could be said as well that my mother began to write this play a long time ago when we were growing up and she decided to keep her diaries. She became a reporter, recording all the funny things, the awkwardness of our lives, the homesickness, the unexplainable stuff which she could not even tell her own people back home. And maybe that is when I began writing this story, one night when I woke up with a nightmare and my mother got me to draw it out on paper. My fingers were too sleepy even to hold the pen. But she waited patiently until I was finished. And here it is, that strange, big-eyed, scary shape of childhood, drawn out for the theatre.

Hugo Hamilton
September 2011

The Speckled People was first performed at the Gate Theatre, Dublin, on 4 October 2011. The production featured the following cast and creatives:

Boy (Hanni)	Tadhg Murphy
Mother (Irmgard)	Julika Jenkins
Father (Seán) / Sailor	Denis Conway
Aunty Eily	Marion O'Dwyer
Gearóid	John Kavanagh
Stiegler	Stephen Brennan
Shopkeeper	Tom Hickey
Bully Boy 1	John Cronin
Bully Boy 2	Jonathan Delaney Tynan

Director Patrick Mason
Set and costume designer Joe Vanek
Lighting designer Davy Cunningham
Composer and sound designer Philip Stewart

The author would like to thank Patrick Mason for his extraordinarily generous assistance in the development of this play for the stage.

Characters

Boy (Hanni) – *Dressed in short trousers, played by an actor in his early twenties.*

Mother (Irmgard) – *German; a warm-hearted young mother in her early thirties, wearing German fashions.*

Father (Seán) – *Irish; an idealistic man in his mid thirties. He speaks with a country accent, wears round glasses and walks with a limp.*

Aunty Eily
Gearóid
Stiegler
Shopkeeper
Bully Boy 1⎫
Bully Boy 2⎭ *Both wear short trousers*
Sailor

Dublin. Ireland in the 1950s.

The stage is sparsely furnished – writing desk to the left with a small radio. There is a single bed at the centre upstage and a wardrobe further back with a single suitcase on top. To the right of the stage a single armchair and gramophone record player.

The play is written in such a way that it can also be produced with six players, allowing the Bully Boys to take on the following roles:

Bully Boy 1 / Stiegler / Gearóid
Bully Boy 2 / Shopkeeper

Act One

Spotlight comes up on the **Boy**, *facing the audience at the front of the stage.* **Mother** *upstage left.* **Father** *upstage right.*

Boy   When you're small you know nothing.

Mother   *Wenn du klein bist, weisst du nichts.*

Father   *Nuair a bhíonn tú óg ní thuigeann tú faic.*

Boy   You don't know who you are, or where you are, or what questions to ask.

Mother   *Du weisst nicht wer du bist oder wo du bist oder welche Fragen du stellen sollst.*

Father   *Níl a fhios agat cé leat thú, ná cá bhfuil tú, ná cén sórt ceisteanna ba chóir duit a chur.*

Boy   When I was small I woke up in Germany. Then I looked out the window and saw Ireland. My mother speaks German and my father speaks Irish and outside the front door is another country where they speak English. I can see the gardener across the street clipping the hedge in English. I can see the boys going by on their way to the football field, but we don't play with them because they don't speak any Irish and we're not allowed to speak any English.

Father   *Nuair a bhíonn tú óg ní thuigeann rud ar bith.*

Mother   *Wenn du klein bist, weisst du gar nichts.*

Boy   One day when I was playing football with my brother and sister at the seafront, I fell over a man lying on his back with his mouth open. He sat up and said, 'Jaysus, what the Jaysus.' I told my mother and father that the man said Jaysus what the Jaysus in English, but they started laughing at the sea. My father was blinking through his glasses and my mother had her hand over her mouth, laughing and laughing until the tears came into her eyes and I thought, maybe she's not laughing at all but crying.

How do know what that means when her shoulders are shaking and she can't talk?

Father *leaves.* **Mother** *carries a parcel onstage.*

Mother   Franz! Hanni! Maria!

Boy   How do you know if she's happy or sad?

Mother   Children. Come quickly.

Boy   And how do you know if your father is happy or whether he's still angry at all the things that are not finished yet in Ireland?

Mother *carries the parcel to the centre of the stage.* **Boy** *joins her.*

Mother   Look. We've got a parcel.

Boy   Is it from home?

Mother   Yes. From Kempen.

Mother *kneels down and begins to open the parcel.*

Imagine that. I came over to Ireland to send home food parcels to Germany after the war. Now the parcels are coming here instead.

She begins to unpack the items with great care, laying them neatly.

Now. Let's see what they've sent us this time. Look. A new story book for you. And a book about chess for your father. Chocolate. And biscuits. And a bottle of Cognac. These chocolate angels must be for Christmas. Look at all these lovely clothes.

Holds up a pair of German lederhosen.

Would you believe it. Lederhosen.

Boy   What's that?

Mother   German trousers. Made of pure leather. All the boys wear them in Germany. Here, let's put them on straight away.

*She takes off the **Boy**'s trousers to put on the lederhosen.*

They last for ever. You'll be indestructible.

Boy   What's indestructible?

Mother   Indestructible. Unbreakable. You'll be able to fall on nails and sit on nettles. You'll be able to slide down granite rocks and climb on trees and nothing will hurt you.

Boy   So nobody can execute me.

Mother   Why would they do that?

Boy   Because I'm a Nazi.

Mother   Who says that?

Boy   The boys going up to the football field.

Mother   Don't listen to them, Hanni.

Boy   They call us Hitler and Goering.

Mother   Nonsense.

Boy   Gestapo. SS. Larry Eichmann.

Mother   They have no idea.

Boy   They say I'm going to be executed.

Mother   Listen to me. Your Onkel Gerd stood up to the Nazis. He was the Lord Mayor of Kappellen and they threw him out of office because he refused to swear an oath to Hitler.

Boy   What's an oath?

Mother   That's when you put your hand on your heart and make a promise. If you say NO inside your head, the promise doesn't count.

Boy   No.

Mother   It's called the silent negative.

Boy   Inside my head.

Mother   I promise with my hand on my heart that I will –
NOT – obey Hitler.

Boy (*hand on his heart*)   I promise that I am – NOT – a Nazi.

Mother   When you get married you make a promise as
well. I came over here to Ireland after the war and made a
promise to your father.

Boy   What promise?

Mother   I promised that I would love him and that I would
be a good mother and not argue too much.

Boy   They promised to kill me.

Mother   They're always making promises they can't keep.

Boy *is utterly puzzled now.* **Mother** *takes his hands in hers.*

Hanni. Listen. You know the dog down at the seafront that
barks at the waves.

Boy   The dog that belongs to nobody.

Mother   Yes. Well the reason he keeps barking at the waves
all day is that he doesn't know any better. So don't let them
tell you that you're a Nazi, because it's not true. They just
don't know any better.

Mother *lets go of his hands and leans back to admire the* **Boy** *in his
new trousers. She claps her hands together, up to her chin.*

I can't believe my own eyes.

Boy   Why not?

Mother   Look at you.

Boy *looks at his new trousers.*

I think I'm back home in Kempen again. Next thing I'll be
sending you over to the bakery for the bread rolls.

Boy   Across the Buttermarkt square.

Mother   You know the way already.

Boy   Past the Sankt Georg fountain.

Mother   But you haven't been there yet.

Boy   Next to the cinema.

Mother   When I was a girl I looked out the window one day and everything had changed. I saw a thousand Nazis with flags and torches on the Buttermarkt square. And I knew what was coming.

Boy   You have to carry the cakes flat, with two hands underneath.

She throws her arms around the **Boy** *and holds him closely.*

Mother   My little teddy bear.

Boy   Mutti. You're cracking my bones.

She laughs and lets him go.

My mother makes everything better with cakes and kisses and hugs that crack your bones.

Mother *picks up the items off the floor and goes to the writing desk. The* **Boy** *watches her as she switches on the radio. The song 'Magic Moments' plays as she stores the items from the parcel away.*

My mother's name is Irmgard and she was trapped in a bad film once that happened in Germany long ago. She says it was like being in a black-and-white picture that you couldn't get out of. With lots of war and trains on fire. She was not allowed to listen to the radio in English, because the Nazis made a rule that you could not believe anything that was said by the enemy.

Mother *sings along with the song.*

Mother (*singing*)   Magic Moments . . .

Boy   She likes to sing along to the words so she can learn English and talk to the people outside in Ireland.

Mother (*singing*)   When two hearts are sharing.

Boy   My father comes from the town of Leap in West Cork and he's got one soft foot and one hard foot. If he hears any of the enemy words from England coming into the house he will switch us off like the radio.

Boy *watches as the* **Father** *enters, wearing a cap and carrying a briefcase and a small parcel in the other hand. He takes off his cap, listening with a stern expression. He drops his briefcase with a clack.*

Mother   Magic. . .

Mother *rushes to switch off the radio. Silence.* **Father** *walks to the centre of the stage with the parcel.* **Mother** *comes to kiss him.*

Father   Wait till you see this, Irmgard.

Boy   Another parcel, Mutti.

Father (*holds up the parcel*)   Something Irish this time.

Boy   An Irish surprise.

Father   To match those German leather britches.

Mother   Trousers.

Father   Trousers. Trousers. Trousers.

Father *unties the parcel.*

Mother   Am I being too fussy?

Father   No. No. Please. You're a great teacher, Irmgard.

Mother   It's the only way to learn German. Correcting every mistake.

Father   I have plenty of mistakes left to make.

Mother   You are my best student, Seán.

Father   Now.

Father *opens the parcel.* **Boy** *looks in.*

Boy   What is that?

Father *reveals a white Aran sweater.*

Father   The Aran sweater.

Mother   My goodness, Hanni. You'll be even more indestructible.

Father *begins to put the Aran sweater on the* **Boy**.

Boy   So nobody can laugh at me.

Father   They can laugh all they like. You are the genuine article. Made in Ireland

Mother   I'll have to write this down into my diary.

Father   Pure wool.

Mother   Wait till they hear this in Kempen.

Father   You see, one day you'll wake up and wonder what country you're living in.

Mother   You think he might forget.

Father   Your history is your place. When I was a boy I looked out the window and saw Michael Collins stopping on the street outside. The same day he was killed in an ambush.

Mother (*puzzled*)   Your history is your place?

Father   Place of origin. Where you come from.

Mother   Would it not be better to say your home?

Father   Exactly. Your history is your home and your language is your home and you'd be lost without your own language.

Boy   But people are laughing at us.

Father   There's always somebody laughing in Ireland.

Mother   He's half and half now. Irish on top and German below.

Father   Brack.

Mother   What's that?

Father   It's the Irish for speckled.

Mother   Brack.

Father   Mixed up. Coloured. Like a speckled trout.

Boy   Barm brack.

Father   With raisins in it.

Boy   For Halloween.

Mother (*pause*)   Speckled Irish cake with German raisins.

Father   Wait till they see you going into the shop to buy sweets.

Boy   Fruit gums, please.

Father (*slaps the* **Boy** *on the back of the head*)   Irish.

Mother   But they don't have those sweets in Gaelic.

Father   Irish. Irish. Irish.

Boy   Gummy.

Mother   Seán, the shopkeeper doesn't speak any Irish.

Father   Well he better learn it.

Boy   Fruity Gummy.

Father   Gummy Gummy.

Mother   Gummy, Gaelic. I'll never get the pronunciation right.

Boy   Gummy gummy fruity fruity gummy fruity.

Father (*suddenly turning on the audience*)   It's not a dead language.

Mother   It's like toffee in my mouth.

Father (*to* **Mother**)   And it's not toffee either.

Mother   As long as we understand each other, that's all that matters.

Father   There is no English in this house.

Mother   You mean there is no English to be heard in this house.

Boy   Only German or Irish.

Father   Only German or Irish.

Mother   To be heard.

Father (*raising his voice*)   There will be no English spoken under this roof. Is that clear?

Silence. **Father** *sits down in his armchair and picks up his book.*

Boy   My father makes all the rules in our house. My mother can't break the rules, so she tells us to go down to the seafront and find the dog that barks at the waves all day.

Mother (*tidying the boy's collar*)   Off you go now.

Boy   I am Adolf Hitler and I'm going down to the shops.

Mother   But that's impossible.

Boy   I'm a Nazi and I'm going to buy fruit gummies.

Mother   No. You can't be a Nazi.

Boy   Sieg Heil.

Mother   I'll cry if you say that.

Boy   She is crying because we might fall in between the languages. But I'm going to be as Irish as possible so I don't fall into the dark place between the countries.

Boy *runs off.*

Mother   Sometimes I'm afraid they'll get lost.

Father   The children. They'll be fine.

Mother   They can't speak to anyone. They have no friends. They might as well be in a foreign country.

Father   Don't worry. They'll make themselves understood.

Mother   They might as well be in a foreign country.

Father   They're in the right place as long as they speak their own language.

Mother *is disappointed and walks away to her writing desk. She takes out her diary and begins to write. She turns to face the audience.*

Mother (*writing*)   We're lucky to be alive. There is nothing to be afraid of because we're living in the luckiest place in the world, with no bombs falling and no trains on fire. The sea is like a big glass of blue water filled up to the top. The people are walking along with ice-cream cones and all the sailing boats are flapping like a washing line out in the bay. It's like being on holidays for the rest of your life. Sometimes you forget where you are and who you are. And sometimes you even forget all the things that happened in the past.

We hear a dog barking. Waves crashing. The **Boy** *re-enters, running up to the front of the stage again.*

Boy   Jaysus, will you look at those big waves. Curling in like big bellies. Jumping up like a man in a white suit. Jaysus what the Jaysus, you big bully belly. The dog with no name is barking until he's hoarse and has no voice any more. And we're throwing stones and holding back the enemy words.

He picks up stones and begins to throw them in the direction of the audience.

Get down, you bully belly. Surrender all you bully waves and lie down on the sand with your arms out, because we're Irish and we have our own country and our language is our home.

Boy *freezes as two* **Bully Boys** *appear on the stage left, wearing short trousers.*

Bully Boy 1   Would you look at the Nazi wearing the Aran sweater.

Bully Boy 2   He's a Kraut-Mick.

Bully Boy 1   Séamus Hitler.

Bully Boy 2   Adolf O'Hurlingstick.

Bully Boy 1   Speaking German is even more stupid than speaking Irish.

Bully Boy 2   Hey, that's not your dog.

Bully Boy 1   Let's put him on trial.

Bully Boy 2   Guilty.

Bully Boy 1   For stealing the dog with no name.

Bully Boy 2   And killing the Jews.

Bully Boy 1   And wearing the Aran sweater.

Bully Boy 2   Yeah. Hiding in Ireland with your Nazi Ma.

Bully Boy 1   Execute him.

Bully Boy 2   Execute him.

The **Bully Boys** *hit the* **Boy** *and run off offstage.*

Boy   Mutti. Mutti.

Mother *looks up from the table.*

Mother   What's wrong?

Boy   I'm not indestructible.

Mother (*stands up*)   Now calm down and tell me what happened.

Boy   They said I have a Nazi mother.

Mother   Seán. Come and listen to this. It's those boys going up to the football field.

Father (*sitting down*)   What did they say?

Boy   They have ways of making us talk.

Father   English?

Boy   Yes.

Father   Did you talk?

Boy   No.

Father   You said nothing.

Boy   They spoke German.

Father   What?

Boy   Donner und Blitzen. Schweinhund.

Father   Ignore them. Their heads are full of rubbish from British comics.

Boy   They're going to execute us.

Father   How?

Boy   Sieg Heil. Mahogany gas pipe.

Father   Complete nonsense.

Mother (*to* **Father**)   Let him speak.

Mother *and* **Father** *watch the* **Boy** *running around in circles.*

Boy   Sieg Heil. Donner und Blitzen. Gott in himmel schweinhund. Achtung. Achtung. Schnell schnell. Himmel and blitzen Nazi, Séamus Hitler and Rippentrop and donner und Schplitter, scheisse. Panzer. Goering. Akakakakakakakak, Jaysus what the Jaysus. Himmel Schwein. aaaaaaaaaaaaargh.

The **Boy** *falls down miming an agonising death. Silence.*

Father   It's full of mistakes.

Mother   They speak with their fists.

Boy   Eeeek. Aaaargh, Messerschmidt. Aus-witch.

Silence. **Mother** *and* **Father** *look at each other. The* **Boy** *lies motionless on the floor.*

Father   Have nothing to do with them. They get all that Nazi language from the British.

Father *takes a document from his briefcase and reads it.* **Mother** *left looking at the* **Boy** *on the floor.*

Mother   Come on, get up Hanni. Let's have some chocolate.

Boy *gets up.* **Mother** *leads him over to the writing desk and shares out some chocolate.*

Boy   I tried it, Mutti.

Mother   You tried what?

Boy   The silent negative.

Mother   That's good.

Boy   It doesn't work.

Mother   Oh yes it does. Your aunt, Tante Marianne used the silent negative all through the war. It didn't work for a long time. But then one day a man named Stauffenberg put a bomb in a briefcase to try and kill Hitler. And when everybody was gathered together to hear the news that the Führer was still alive, your Tante Marianne stood up and said, 'What a pity.' It was a very dangerous thing to say. Everybody was sure that she would be arrested and taken away by the Gestapo. But then the woman beside her came to her rescue and said: 'Yes, what a pity such a thing can happen.' So Marianne was saved and went back to the silent negative again. And after that she found a different way of speaking out.

Boy   What a pity I'm not bigger than them.

Mother   You can't fight them, Hanni. They are the fist people and you can't win.

Boy   Because we're guilty?

Mother   You can never say you're innocent.

Boy   What a pity I'm German.

Mother   You can be a good German.

Boy   I want to be Irish.

Mother   You don't want to be like the fist people.

Boy   I promise that I am NOT German.

Mother   You are a lovely, homemade, freshly baked, speckled, Irish-speaking, German. Come on. Bedtime.

The **Boy** *steps back all the way to the far side of the stage. The* **Mother** *opens the bed cover wide and waits.*

One – two – three.

The **Boy** *takes a run and makes an enormous leap into bed, then lies down and she covers him up all in one movement. She sits on the bed and leans down to kiss the boy good night.*

What's that in your hand?

Boy   A stone.

Mother   What for?

Boy   For holding back the bully waves.

Mother   Come on, let Mutti have it.

Boy   I can't.

Mother   Please, let go.

Boy   The grip won't let me.

Mother   Hanni, you can't sleep with that.

Boy   Why not?

Mother   You can't go around for the rest of your life with a stone in your fist.

Boy   It's my stone.

Mother   Let me keep it for you.

Boy   Promise?

Mother   I promise with my hand on my heart that I will keep your stone.

She kisses him again.

Good boy. Off you go to sleep now.

She stands up and walks over to the armchair where the **Father** *is sitting and shows him the stone.*

Look. He was trying to sleep with this in his hand.

Father   He's got nothing to worry about.

Mother   We have nothing to worry about either.

Father   Have you seen this?

Mother   What is it?

Father *gives her the document in his hand. She glances at it.*

Father   We're up to our ears in debt.

Mother   We could have done with that bit of luck.

Father   We need more than luck to fix the boiler.

Mother   Why do they keep turning you down for promotion?

Father   Because I speak Irish. That's why.

Mother   But it's the national language. You work for the electricity supply board. It's a government institution.

Father   You wouldn't understand, Irmgard.

Mother   Do they not like Irish in the office?

Father   It's what this country needs. We need our own culture and our own great inventions.

Mother   Did you say all this to them at the interview?

Father   Of course, I did. I told them exactly where this country was going wrong.

Mother   Then why don't they give you promotion?

Father   Look. We'll just have to find some other way of making extra money.

Mother   I could bake cakes.

Father   Do you have any idea what that boiler will cost?

Mother   Why don't we start a business? Something the Irish people really need.

Father   Where is the credit?

Mother   The capital, you mean.

Father   The capital. The raw materials.

Mother   I'll start a cake factory.

Father   Are you serious?

Mother   Cakes work in any language.

Father   What does language have to do with baking?

Mother   German cakes. Irish ingredients. We'll turn this country around.

Father (*snaps*)   With cakes?

Mother   Why not?

Father   Look. You don't know what was done to the Irish. This country is paralysed. Nobody knows where to begin.

Mother   Seán. You can't bake in anger. Otherwise we will only make an unhappy cake. People will get the taste of doubt. You have to treat the ingredients with affection. You slip the beaten egg into the mixture the way you would slip a love letter into an envelope.

She sits on the side of the chair and puts her arm around the **Father**.

And once the letter is posted and the cake is in the oven, you don't trudge around the house slamming doors. You don't argue and you don't say a bad word about anyone. You whisper, you nod, you tiptoe around the kitchen.

She leans down to kiss him.

Father   If only the Irish could do business like the Germans.

Mother   If only the Germans could laugh like the Irish.

Father   The Irish laugh like there's no tomorrow.

Mother   What a pity Germany and Ireland are not closer to each other.

They are left in a soft pool of light. The **Boy** *sits up, picked out in a spot.*

Boy   I know that my mother and father got married in Germany. At Christmas. With the snow all over. She had no white dress. But the land was all white. And for their honeymoon they went down the Rhine. With all the castles and the fairy tales. They went up the Drachenfels mountain by cable car. They had cake and coffee in a restaurant up there. Then they came back to Ireland and went on the second part of the honeymoon. They climbed up Craugh Patrick. My mother says they had to hold on to the rocks because the wind was so strong. There were some people going up in their bare feet. And there was no restaurant for coffee and cake up there. Only a small church at the top. You had to go around the outside three times saying the rosary. And by the time they got down again it was dark.

The **Mother** *stands up. The* **Father** *puts on his cap and picks up his briefcase.* **Mother** *kisses the* **Father**.

Father   What are you going to call it?

Mother   The cake factory?

Father   You need a strong name. A name that people can trust.

Mother   Mother's cakes.

Father   No English.

Mother   How are they going to know what we're selling?

Father   What's wrong with the Irish name?

Mother   We want to make it easy for people to buy our products.

Father   Once they hear the full-Irish name, they'll never forget it.

Mother   But they have trouble pronouncing it, Seán.

Father   It's our family name.

Mother   They have a different version in every shop.

Father   I have the same problem at the office. But I don't care. I just keep on repeating the name in Irish until I'm blue in the face.

Mother   I'll tell you what. Let's have no name, just a nice blue ribbon.

She watches him as he walks off.

Boy   Now the whole house smells sweet. My mother has started the cake factory and stacked up the production line of cakes and biscuits and jars of chocolate sweets with little blue bows around them on the hall table.

*The **Boy** jumps up and joins the **Mother**. **Mother** and **Boy** pick up baskets and approach the bed, setting down the baskets.*

But the Irish customers don't want anything homemade. They only want things that are made in real factories. Things that look like they cost money to buy. After lots of going in and out of shops and shaking heads and sorry and maybe some other time, we come to the shopkeeper who can't say no and he agrees to take a few cakes and chocolates, just to try them out.

A **Shopkeeper** *appears, wearing a brown coat. He begins to examine the contents of the baskets.* **Mother** *speaks with exaggerated formality.*

Shopkeeper   And where did you learn such good English?

Mother   It is with the intention of learning good English that I came to Ireland.

Shopkeeper   Well, you could give us a few lessons.

Mother   German lessons.

Shopkeeper   No. English lessons.

Mother   That is impossible.

Shopkeeper   I'm not joking you. The way some people talk around here.

Mother   I am full of admiration for the Irish way of speaking English.

Shopkeeper   You wouldn't know what they're blathering about half the time.

Mother   It is full of surprises for me.

Shopkeeper   Must be hard to understand alright.

Mother   No. I can understand everything perfectly. But I can never be sure what Irish people are saying.

Pause. **Shopkeeper** *stares at her for a moment.*

Shopkeeper   Say no more. Now. Who do I make the cheque out to?

Mother   Must it be a cheque?

Shopkeeper   I'm sorry. I have no cash handy.

Mother   The name is O'hUrmoltaigh.

Shopkeeper   That's a bit of a mouthful.

Mother   It's an Irish family name.

Shopkeeper   What's the English for it?

Mother   I have no English name handy.

Shopkeeper   It would make things a lot simpler.

Mother   Let me spell it out for you. Mister . . .

Shopkeeper   Smith.

Mother   Smiss.

Shopkeeper   Smith.

Mother   Smiss.

Boy   Misser Smiss and Misses O'Hurry.

Mother   Stop.

Boy   Misses O'Humming, O'Hubcap, O'Hurlingstick.

Mother   O H U R M . . .

Boy   Misses O'Himmel and Blitzen O'Hurricane.

Mother   Stop it. I have to concentrate.

Boy   Misses O, Misses O, Misses O HUM.

Mother   It would give me great pleasure to write it down for you.

Boy   Misses O.

Shopkeeper   Right. Misses O?

Boy   Missis Oh my God.

Pause. All waiting.

Mother   Hamilton.

Shopkeeper   Ah. Fair play to you.

Mother   Fair play. (*Beat.*) Do you mean justice?

Shopkeeper No. I mean gratitude. Thank you. Fair play to you.

Mother Fair play to YOU.

Shopkeeper Don't mention it.

Mother I will mention it. To my husband.

Pause.

Shopkeeper What's your first name, if you don't mind me asking you?

Mother Irmgard.

Shopkeeper Irmgard. Now there's a perfect name. Irmgard's cakes.

Mother My husband insists on the Irish.

*The **Shopkeeper** hands over the cheque.*

Shopkeeper Well you can tell your husband from me, it's a beautiful language, but it's not great for business.

Mother It has been a great pleasure to do business with you.

Shopkeeper No bother.

Mother Yours sincerely.

*She turns to leave. **Shopkeeper** watches her for a moment before he disappears.*

*As the **Mother** and **Boy** turn back towards the centre of the stage, **Bully Boy 1** and **2** enter right and come marching across the front of the stage past them, raising a Nazi salute.*

Bully Boy 1 Heil Hitler.

Bully Boy 2 Hitler.

Bully Boys *walk off left.* **Mother** *stalls for a moment, then pulls the **Boy** away towards the bed where she sits down to take off her shoes for a moment to rub her feet.*

Mother   Sometimes your feet are your own worst enemy.

Boy   Fifteen shops and three restaurants and two hotels.

Mother   You need a good pair of shoes to do business.

Boy   Two buses and two shortcuts through the lanes.

Mother   It's like going on a pilgrimage.

Boy   And three times sheltering from the rain.

Mother   Worse than Croagh Patrick.

Boy   Did we make a profit?

Mother   Yes.

Boy   Are we going to be rich?

Mother   I'm not so sure. It takes a lot of luck and prayers before you come home with less cakes than you had going out.

Father *returns and clacks his briefcase on the ground.*

Boy (*excited*)   We sold two cakes and two jars of chocolates.

Father   That's a great start, Irmgard.

Mother   I don't think it's cost effective yet.

Father   We need a sound business strategy.

Boy   He said Mutti has very good English.

Father   Who said that?

Boy   The shopkeeper.

Mother   He was just being polite.

Boy   He said Irish was bad for business.

Father   We won't go into his shop any more.

Mother   But he's the only customer we have.

Father *walks over to the* **Mother**.

Boy   Don't forget your fruit gums, chum.

Father (*to* **Boy**)   Stop saying that.

Boy   Don't forget your . . .

Father (*angry*)   Gummy.

Boy   The words are stuck to the roof of my head.

Father (*picking up the cheque*)   What's this?

Mother   I spelled it out for him.

Father   It's in English.

Mother   There was no way out.

Father *tears up the cheque and throws it away.*

Father   He'll have to pay again.

Mother *watches the torn pieces of paper flutter to the floor.*

Boy   Chum chum fruit.

Father (*with increasing rage*)   I told you to stop saying that.

Mother   This makes no sense any more.

Boy   Chum.

Father   Gummy.

Boy   Gummy Chummy.

Father   If you say that again, you're in big trouble.

Boy   Chummy.

Father   Gummy.

Mother   Gaelic.

Father (*shouting*)   Irish.

Boy   Gummy, Gummy, Fruity, Chummy.

Father *suddenly turns on the* **Boy** *and strikes him.*

Father (*shouting*)　Speak your own language.

The **Boy** *goes head over heels across the stage and lands head first. The* **Mother** *runs over to him and picks him up. She looks back at the* **Father**.

Mother　Now, why did you do that?

The **Mother** *tends to the* **Boy**'s *nose.*

Father　He has to stick to the rules.

Mother　He's bleeding.

Father　He won't listen.

Mother　You broke his nose.

Father　Well he knows the rules now.

Mother　My God, Seán.

Father　I've got a lot of work to do in the garden.

Father *rolls up his sleeves and limps away.* **Mother** *examines the* **Boy**'s *nose.*

Mother　Come here. Poor teddy bear. Let's have a look. Hold still. (*Cleaning him up.*) We'll have to fix your nose with a bit of chocolate.

She embraces him and looks towards the audience.

Boy　Mutti. You're cracking my bones.

Mother *lets him go and strokes his head.*

Mother　Come on.

Mother *pulls down the suitcase from the top of the wardrobe.*

Boy　Where are we going?

Mother　We can't let this happen again.

Boy　Are we going home?

Mother　We got trapped before in Germany. We waited until it was too late. If we don't go now we'll be right back where it started and there is nothing we can do to stop it.

Boy   Home to the Buttermarkt square?

Mother   We'll have no courage left to say no.

Mother *takes the* **Boy** *by the hand and leads him away.*

Boy   Is Papa one of the fist people?

Mother   Come on. Let's go.

Boy   Good bye house. Good bye garden.

Mother *stops at the writing desk and picks up her diary.*

Mother   Don't look back.

Boy   Good bye waves. Good bye dog. Good bye barking. Good bye, good bye, good bye, good bye.

Mother *and* **Boy** *walk away off stage.*

Silence. The stage is empty.

The **Father** *re-enters and looks around.*

Father   Irmgard.

Father *limps around the stage searching.*

Irmgard.

Father *stands at the centre of the stage alone.*

Where are you?

Father *becomes aware that the suitcase is gone and limps off in a hurry.*

The stage is left empty.

Mother *and* **Boy** *appear right, walking briskly across the stage. As they reach the left side, the* **Father** *re-enters and finally catches up with them.*

Irmgard. Irmgard. Please.

Mother *stops and turns around to face him.*

Where are you going?

Mother　We can't stay here.

Father　But where would you go?

Mother　Home.

Father　Your home is here.

Mother　I have no home.

Father　You're married, Irmgard.

Mother　The children are afraid.

Father　I lost my temper.

Mother　They won't forget this.

Father　I don't know what came over me.

Mother　You always have to win. (*Gathering force.*) You never give in. You have us like soldiers. In this language war. We don't know what to say any more. You lay down all these rules in the house. And when he breaks the rules you break his nose.

Father　I'll change, Irmgard. I promise.

Mother　I don't want my children emigrating every time they walk out the front door. I don't want them flinching all the time and fighting with the rest of the world.

Father　I'm trying to do my best. For you. For my children. For Ireland.

Mother　You can't even say you're sorry.

Mother *turns and leads the* **Boy** *away off stage.*

Father　I beg you, Irmgard. Come back. (*Pause.*) Irmgard.

Father *stands alone on the stage.*

We'll go to Connemara.

Silence.

Please. I want to bring you to Connemara, to a place called
the red quarter. Where everything is red and brown. As far
as the eye can see. Full of bogs and silence. (*Beat.*) And rocks.
And Irish.

Pause.

Everywhere.

Pause.

To be heard.

Pause

Irmgard.

*He turns to face the audience. He takes off his glasses and wipes
them, staring ahead.* **Mother** *and* **Boy** *appear once more behind
him. She places the suitcase on the floor.*

Mother   I have nowhere to go.

Father *turns around and goes to her.*

Father   I'll take you home.

Father *picks up the suitcase and gently leads her by the arm.*

(*to the* **Boy**) She's just a bit homesick, that's all.

They make their way slowly back towards the armchair. The **Father**
puts the suitcase down and helps the **Mother** *into the armchair. She
is still holding the diary in her hands.*

We'll put on some music. German music.

He turns to the **Boy**.

Hanni. You go on up to bed now.

The **Boy** *stalls.* **Father** *gives the boy a sweet.*

Here's an Irish toffee. Everything is alright. Think about the
future. About Connemara.

Look. I'm sorry about your nose. I didn't mean it. I just
want you to be stronger. More indestructible. I want you to
be able to stand up to the bullies on the street. I had all that

when I was a boy. They kept laughing at me about my limp and calling me Hopalong. You can't show any weakness. You have to be strong all the time.

Boy *accepts the sweet but remains standing there.*

Off you go now. One two three.

Boy *walks away and sits on the bed.* **Father** *rushes over to the gramophone.*

Let me see now. Ah yes. Elisabeth Schwarzkopf. The greatest voice ever. (*Beat.*) To be heard.

Elisabeth Schwarzkopf singing 'Leise, Leise, Fromme Weise' – from Der Freischutz, *by Weber. As the music comes up, the* **Father** *stalls for a moment with his fingers in the air, an expression of ecstasy. He goes over to the* **Mother** *and sits down on the floor beside her.*

This is your place, Irmgard.

She is in a dream. He takes her hand and places it around his shoulder. He rests his head against her knee.

The music fills the whole house.

Boy   I know that my grandmother was an opera singer. She sang at the Krefeld opera house. And the men who wanted to marry her all sent bouquets of flowers on to the stage after each performance. But then my grandfather, Franz Kaiser, sent a basket of bananas into her dressing room instead. So that was it. That's how they got married.

Mother *stands up and walks slowly over to the writing desk. She places her diary back on the desk. Then she goes over to sit on the bed and covers the* **Boy** *up. The music continues.*

Mother   Your grandfather was a businessman. He owned a stationery shop on the Buttermarkt square. There was a big metal quill over the door, with his name. Franz Kaiser. He was a very funny man and the people loved him. But then the crash came. Nobody had any money. The shop had to be closed.

When he was dying I had to bring him a mirror so that he could say good bye to himself. Auf Wiedersehen, Franz, he said. I was only nine years of age when he died. Your grandmother taught piano lessons to keep things going. But they loved each other too much and she died because she was not able to live without him. Then we all moved in with Tante Maria and Onkel Gerd, the Lord Mayor. And when the Nazis came to power, he was thrown out of office for objecting to Hitler and I had to leave school. I got a job in Düsseldorf, working in an office. I was only sixteen.

The **Boy** *has fallen asleep.*

Then I got trapped. I didn't know how to escape. And I heard the footsteps of Herr Stiegler coming up the stairs.

The spot fades down on her and the music fades out.

End of Act One.

Act Two

Out of the dark, the **Boy** *wakes up from a nightmare, picked out in a spot.*

Boy No. No. No. Mutti. Mutti.

Mother Hanni.

Boy No.

Mother *enters.*

Mother I'm coming.

Boy I didn't do it.

Mother *rushes over towards the bed.*

Mother What's the matter?

Boy They said I killed people.

Mother *sits on the bed and hugs the* **Boy**.

Mother It's just a bad dream, that's all.

Boy Dead hands. And dead eyes, Mutti.

Mother It's OK. Hanni. You're here, in Ireland. (*Beat.*) I'll tell you what we'll do. Come on. Up you get.

Mother *gets the* **Boy** *out of bed and brings him over to the writing desk. She sits him down, then leans over him.*

I'm going to give you the pen so you can draw out the nightmare for me.

Boy Now?

Mother While you still remember it.

She hands him the pen.

Boy I can't push.

Mother Take your time.

Boy   My fingers are too soft.

Mother   Sleepy fingers. Come on, let me help you.

Mother *takes his hand and they begin to draw.*

Boy   Big monster.

Mother   With spikes.

Boy   And smoke out of his mouth.

Mother   And trains on fire.

Boy   And dead people.

Mother   And all their suitcases.

Boy   And dead eyes.

Mother   Eyes with no more tears. Nothing more they can bear to see. Only a silent question left inside and no answer.

Boy   And you over here.

Mother   With my blue dress.

Boy   And your arms out.

Mother   Right across the page.

Boy   Laughing or crying?

Mother   Laughing.

Boy   Laughing and laughing until the tears come.

Mother *gives the* **Boy** *a big kiss on the side of his face.*

Mother   There you are. Your nightmare is drawn out on paper.

She closes over the diary and strokes the **Boy**'s *head.*

Now you'll be able to sleep.

Boy   It won't come back?

Mother   I'm going to keep it here in my diary. Right next to my nightmare.

Boy   Like a nightmare factory.

Mother   Our nightmare factory.

Boy   Does everybody have nightmares?

Mother   Everybody.

Boy   Papa too.

Mother   Sometimes.

Boy   Does he draw them out?

Mother   He writes letters. To the Government.

Boy   About the bullies?

Mother   What bullies?

Boy   The bully boys are after him and he's got a limp and he can't run away.

Mother   Hanni. Your father has a weakness and they were cruel to him when he was a boy. Now. Off you go, back to sleep. One-two-three.

*She holds up the bed covers and the **Boy** leaps into bed again. She sits on the edge of the bed and tucks him in.*

Boy   Will I get the weakness?

Mother   Everybody has their own weakness.

Boy   Will I get the limp?

Mother   No. You have nothing to worry about. We'll soon be going to Connemara.

Boy   Is that in the future?

Mother   Yes. The future as far as the eye can see. Like walking on the moon. Your father says it's full of emptiness. And rocks. And Irish. Yes. And silver beaches with no footprints on them yet. And at night it's all darkness and tiny lights and dogs barking into infinity.

*The **Boy** is asleep again. She kisses him on the forehead and stands up. She goes back to the desk and sits down. She picks up the pen, ready to write in her diary.*

Now we have the nightmare factory in our house. Nightmares in Irish and nightmares in German and nightmares in English outside the front door. Everybody has their own nightmares. Everybody has their own weakness. Everybody has their own bully to deal with.

Stiegler *appears carrying a file.*

Stiegler   Heil Hitler.

Mother *fumbles with a pen to avoid the salute.*

Mother   Heil NOT.

Stiegler *stands facing her, looking at the file in his hand.*

Stiegler   This is very unsatisfactory, Fraülein Kaiser. Quite honestly. Your work is a complete mess. Mistakes everywhere.

Mother   I'm sorry, Herr Stiegler.

Stiegler   Sloppy. Slow. Incompetent.

Mother   I'm only new here.

Stiegler   From Kempen. I know. Your uncle was the Lord Mayor of Kapellen.

Mother   I promise I will improve.

Stiegler *takes a moment to examine her.*

Stiegler   The hair is an improvement.

Mother   I beg your pardon.

Stiegler   Your hair. Looks good. Nice style. Stand up.

Mother *stands up.* **Stiegler** *walks all around her, looking her up and down.*

Not bad. (*Pause.*) Your figure is one thing you have going for you.

Mother (*objecting*)   Herr Stiegler.

Stiegler   Your mother sang at the opera.

Mother   Yes. The Krefeld Opern Haus.

Stiegler   What did she sing?

Mother   Weber. Mozart. Everything really.

Stiegler   I have a spare ticket for Saturday night.

Mother   You are married, Herr Stiegler.

Stiegler   What does that mean?

Mother   I couldn't.

Stiegler   My wife and I would like to invite you to join us at the opera. Does that sound any better?

Mother   Thank you, Herr Stiegler.

Stiegler   As long as I see some improvement.

Stiegler *disappears.* **Mother** *sits down again with her diary.* **Boy** *sits up in bed.*

The **Father** *is busy working on a German handcart, tapping it with a hammer.*

Boy   My father and mother tried lots of different things that didn't work. They tried to make extra money by selling metal stands for Christmas trees. They imported hand-carved crucifixes but nobody needs any more crosses in Ireland.

Now my father is starting a new factory. He knows what the people of Ireland need most, so he makes wooden trains and wooden cars. And stilts.

Father *pulls the handcart up to the front of the stage, centre.*
Mother *sits writing in her diary.*

Mother   Main components – six shillings. Wheels, with duty – two shillings and six pence. Paint – one shilling. Screws etcetera – six pence. Rope – eight pence. Glue and plastic wood – three pence. Wood for blocks – six pence. Labour – five shillings. Overheads at 12½ per cent – two shillings and a penny.

Father   What does that come to?

Mother   Eighteen shillings and three pence.

Father   I can't make them any cheaper than that.

Mother   Can we sell them at nineteen?

Father   That would be giving it away, Irmgard. It's not every day you see a well-made German handcart around here.

Mother   We have to remain competitive.

Father   How can we compete? Anyone can build a boxcar, out of scrap. It's a waste of time, carrying that thing around with me.

Mother   Nothing is wasted.

Father   I'm trying to get the country on its feet. Everyone laughing at me.

Mother   They have better things to laugh at.

Father   They're laughing because I built that wooden cart for no good reason.

She kisses him while he stares ahead with great determination.

Mother   We'll put it under the Christmas tree. For the children.

Father   But we've gained nothing.

Mother   You mean, we've made no profit.

Father   Profit. Profit. Profit.

Mother   You're such a good father. Look at all the toys you've made for them. Everything in wood. None of that cheap plastic stuff.

Father   Imported rubbish. That's all they want. Letting the country down every time.

Mother   Our children don't know how lucky they are. You're so devoted. You never go out to the pub like other men. Laughing and joking and having a good time. (*Beat.*) Come on. Christkind. Let's get everything laid out.

Father (*stalls*)   The family is the strongest institution.

Mother   That's our profit.

They begin to prepare for Christmas. **Father** *brings a Christmas tree on stage.* **Mother** *carries chocolates and biscuits over to place them into the handcart. She drapes a sheet over the handcart. The* **Father** *hanging decorations on the tree. The* **Boy** *sits up in bed.*

Boy   When I was small I looked out the window and everything was covered over with snow. The whole country was silent and we were all back home in Germany again. My mother says the snow turns everybody into children, even my father.

Mother   The music, Seán.

Father   Music. Music. Music.

Boy   Everything in our house is German now. All the toys and the sweets are spread out on the carpet.

The Christmas tree is now lit up, simulating white candles. The **Father** *runs like a child with great excitement over to the gramophone.*

Mother   Ready.

Boy   Ready.

Father   Ready. Bells and bells and German bells.

We hear the sound of bells from the Cologne Cathedral.

Boy   The bells are ringing and the candles on the tree are spluttering and the snow outside is falling.

Mother   Now children. See what Christkind has brought you.

The **Boy** *comes rushing forward to see the cart in the middle of the stage. He lifts the sheet and discovers the handcart.*

Boy (*surprise*)   Look Mutti. A hand cart.

Father *puts his arm around the* **Mother** *as they watch the boy. We hear the Cologne Children's Choir singing 'Ihr Kinderlein Kommet'.*

Mother   It feels like being at home.

Father   You are at home.

Mother   Where I belong.

Father   This is where you belong.

Mother   Where the children are happy and where the postman brings my letters and where the bells of the Cologne Cathedral are ringing all the way across the sea to Ireland.

The **Boy** *gets into the cart and eats chocolate.* **Father** *places the* **Mother** *into the armchair once more. He then places his hand on her shoulder.*

Boy   How do you know what your mother is thinking. How do you know if she is here in Ireland or far away at home with all the things that she remembers about Germany long ago.

Stiegler *crosses the stage. The* **Mother** *stands up and freezes.* **Stiegler** *disappears.*

Aunty Eily *appears. A strong-willed, older woman with a Cork accent.* **Father** *goes to greet her.*

Aunty Eily   Is this the cake factory?

Father   Aunty Eily. It's good to see you.

Aunty Eily (*inhaling*)   The smell of baking is such a great welcome.

Boy   When Aunty Eily comes to visit us, we're back in Ireland again. The house is full of smoke and English and there is nothing my father can do about it because Aunty Eily is from Skibbereen and she can't speak any German, or Irish.

Aunty Eily   You haven't changed a bit, Jack.

Father   It's Seán.

Aunty Eily (*turning to* **Mother**)   Irmgard.

Mother   It's very kind of you to come and visit us.

Aunty Eily   They're all talking about you down in West Cork.

Mother   Why is that?

Aunty Eily   The cakes, of course.

Father   The great German kitchen.

Aunty Eily   The great Irish appetite.

Mother   It is a tragedy that cakes cannot be sent by post.

Aunty Eily   Never a truer word spoken, Irmgard.

Aunty Eily *gives a box of jelly sweets to the* **Boy**.

Now Hanni. Will you share these out.

Boy *puts them into the cart and continues eating chocolate.*

Father   Aunty Eily. You shouldn't have.

Aunty Eily   They're only shop bought.

Mother   What do you say, Hanni?

The **Boy** *hesitates and looks at his* **Father** *first.*

Boy   Gummy, Aunty Eily.

Aunty Eily   You're very gummy welcome, boy.

Mother *gives* **Aunty Eily** *a glass of cognac.* **Aunty Eily** *sits down.*

Mother   Did the snow fall on to Skibbereen too?

Aunty Eily   Honest to God, Irmgard. I've never seen so much snow before in my life.

Mother   Everything is brand new white.

Aunty Eily   You wouldn't know where you were.

Father   It's like a different country.

Aunty Eily   All the way up on the train, I thought I was abroad.

Boy   When Aunty Eily talks in English, my father has to answer in English. And maybe he's a nicer man with his soft Cork accent, because that's the language his mother spoke when he was small. English was the language she had for his bedtime stories.

Aunty Eily   Was Santa good to you, Hanni?

Father   I'm afraid we don't have Santa in this house, Aunty Eily.

Mother (*defusing*)   Christkind.

Aunty Eily (*to the* **Boy**)   What did you get for Christmas?

They look at the **Boy**.

Boy   But I don't know what language to give my answer in. I have to translate all the words in my head and they get mixed up in three languages. I have to look over my shoulder to see what country I'm in before I speak.

Mother (*to the* **Father**)   He wants to know if he can answer in English.

Father   I suppose he has no alternative.

Mother (*to the* **Boy**)   Go ahead.

Boy (*hesitant*)   A German handcart . . . for Christmas . . . we got.

Everyone staring at the **Boy**. *Silence.* **Aunty Eily** *is friendly but firm.*

Aunty Eily   I know it's Christmas, Jack. But only your own people will tell you this. It's wrong what you're doing. Not letting your children speak English in their own country.

Father   My name is not Jack. It's Seán.

Aunty Eily   You'll turn them against you.

Father   We all have to make sacrifices.

Aunty Eily   They're like strangers in their own home, Jack. They're afraid to open their mouths.

Father   They have their own language. They'll appreciate it later.

Aunty Eily   But your own father didn't speak any Irish.

Father   My father died in the wrong language.

Aunty Eily   Your father was a lovely man, Jack.

Father   He fought for the British when his own country was still not free.

Aunty Eily   He was injured and lost his memory.

Father   On a British battleship.

Aunty Eily   More homesick than seasick. That's what he wrote on his last postcard.

Boy   One day we found the picture of a sailor in the wardrobe.

Aunty Eily   Your mother kept his picture over the mantelpiece.

Boy   We got into the wardrobe and pretended it was a bus. Then it fell over and we got trapped inside with the sailor.

Aunty Eily   I saw her holding his uniform in her arms, long after he was buried.

Boy   The sailor with the soft eyes.

Father   We can't feel sad for the people who died on the wrong side.

Father *walks briskly towards the right side of the stage.*

Aunty Eily   How can you turn your back on your own father?

Boy   My father pulled us out of the wardrobe and then he locked the door. For ever.

Mother (*to* **Aunty Eily**)   More homesick than seasick?

Aunty Eily   That's right, Irmgard. More homesick than seasick.

Gearóid *enters right, a flamboyant character, in an Irish way.*

Gearóid   God bless the full-Irish fireside.

Father   Ah Gearóid. A hundred thousand welcomes. You couldn't have come at a better time.

Gearóid (*to the* **Mother**)   A Christmas of true Irish happiness and prosperity to you all.

Mother   I'm sorry.

Gearóid   Much Christmas happiness be with you.

Mother   I beg your pardon.

Boy (*to the* **Mother**)   He's saying happy Christmas.

Mother   Many happy returns to you, (*trouble pronouncing the name*) Gearóid.

Gearóid (*to the* **Father**)   Does she not speak?

Father   It's not on her tongue.

Gearóid   Did you not teach her?

Father   She has trouble chewing the language.

Gearóid   Not a blessed word.

Father   It's a problem, I know. But it can't be helped.

Gearóid   We are forced to speak the enemy tongue.

Father   I'm afraid so.

Aunty Eily (*to the* **Mother**)   I don't speak it either, Irmgard.

Mother (*to* **Aunty Eily**)   I can't pronounce gummy.

Aunty Eily   I'm hopeless. Irmgard. Absolutely HOPELESS.

Pause. **Gearóid** *gives the* **Mother** *a jar of honey.*

Gearóid   Pure Irish honey.

Mother   You are very kind. Fair play to you.

Gearóid   I got it straight from the beekeeper.

Mother   You shouldn't have.

Gearóid   He's an Irish speaker.

Mother   You are not serious?

Gearóid   A native speaker.

Mother   Native Irish honey.

Boy (*in his own world*)   Hopeless.

Father *glances at the* **Boy,** *then gives* **Gearóid** *a glass of brandy.*

Father   Some German brandy.

Mother   Cognac.

Father   German cognac.

Boy   Absolutely. Hopeless.

Father *again glances at the* **Boy.**

Gearóid   Did you get the promotion, Seán?

Father   No. But I didn't back down either.

Gearóid   That's good.

Father   I gave the people of Mullingar a choice. I told them I didn't care if they were left in darkness for another hundred years. I was not going to get their electricity switched back on again until they agreed to write my name in Irish.

Gearóid   Well done, Seán. That's leadership.

Aunty Eily   I'm glad I don't live in Mullingar.

Mother   Thank God.

Pause. **Father** *looks irritated.*

Gearóid   Do you know what, Seán. There could be something in it for you. This beekeeping.

Father   That's a great idea, Gearóid.

Gearóid   Very productive business. The man I got that honey from says he can't keep up with the demand.

Mother (*sceptical*)   Bees?

Gearóid   Think of it. A factory producing honey.

Mother   With all the children around?

Gearóid   No overheads, Seán. The raw materials are all out there in the gardens. Flowers. Blossoms. Fruit trees. All those bees working for you. Travelling up to ten miles in every direction to bring in the honey. You don't have to tell them what to do. You don't have to pay them any wages. And they won't just get up and emigrate either.

Aunty Eily   Unless they swarm.

Gearóid   There's a way of dealing with that, too, Seán. If you talk to them. It's an ancient custom, talking to the bees.

Aunty Eily   In Irish, I suppose.

Mother (*laughs*) Honest to God.

Gearóid You tell the bees everything.

Father That's the new factory for us, Irmgard. The beehive.

Mother We will be forced to close all the windows.

Gearóid In the spring. That's the time to start.

Aunty Eily What will the neighbours say?

Mother They will be afraid of bees.

Gearóid Don't worry, Irmgard. They're far more afraid of the Irish language.

Gearóid *and the* **Father** *laugh heartily at this joke.*

Aunty Eily As if you're not isolated enough already.

Gearóid The daily revolution, Seán.

Father The family manifesto.

Gearóid Your country is your family.

Aunty Eily Lucky for Ireland that your party never got into power.

Mother What party?

Aunty Eily Aiseirí. The Resurrection Party. During the war years, Irmgard.

Gearóid What we failed to achieve in public life we will achieve inside the family unit.

Father We tried to get rid of poverty.

Gearóid And unemployment.

Aunty Eily And democracy.

Gearóid We had a great platform.

Aunty Eily You wanted to ban emigration.

Father   We had a great following in Cork.

Aunty Eily   And lipstick.

Mother   Lipstick.

Aunty Eily   Red, Irmgard. The colour of Communism.

Gearóid   The Irish must remain different.

Aunty Eily   What's the use in being different?

Gearóid   We can't be the same as everyone else.

Aunty Eily   We all want the same things, don't we?

Gearóid   The Irish people are unique.

Aunty Eily   We're not the only people who are unique.

Gearóid   But it's great to be Irish.

Aunty Eily   What about Irmgard?

Gearóid   There is no fireside like your own fireside.

Aunty Eily   And no backside like your own backside.

Silence. They all stare at each other.

Look at you, sitting there with the turf smoke coming out of your ears. You've just sent this family back a hundred years with your beekeeping war.

Silence.

Boy (*to himself*)   LIP. STICK.

Silence. **Mother** *attempts to defuse the situation.*

Mother   Maybe we could sing a song?

Aunty Eily   That's a good idea, Irmgard. We've had enough of the daily revolution.

Mother   I have a song handy.

Father   A German song.

Mother   It's a song by Elvis Presley.

Gearóid (*sharp*)   Elvis Presley.

Mother   A German love song.

Aunty Eily   Great.

Mother   The title of the song is 'Wooden Heart'.

Father   'Wooden Heart'?

Mother   We all sang it at home in German. Now Elvis Presley has put new words to it.

Father   English words?

Aunty Eily   Ah for God's sake, Jack. Will you let her sing a song.

Father   She'll sing it in German.

Mother   But Elvis Presley sings it very beautifully.

Gearóid   You can't let her sing that imported rubbish, Seán.

Aunty Eily   You don't have to listen.

Father   Aunty Eily.

Aunty Eily   Irmgard.

Gearóid   Seán.

Father   Irmgard.

Gearóid   The manifesto, Seán.

Aunty Eily   Go ahead, Irmgard. (*Beat.*) Sing it in whatever language you like.

Pause. Everybody waiting.

Mother   Can't you see, I love you, please don't break my heart in two . . .

Gearóid *stands up from his chair abruptly.* **Mother** *stops singing.*

Gearóid   I'm not listening to that jungle music in a full-Irish home.

Aunty Eily   Keep going, Irmgard.

Mother   No bother.

Father   I'm sorry, Gearóid. It's out of my hands.

Gearóid   Strike a blow, Seán. Strike a blow. Elvis Presley has no place in the family unit.

Gearóid *walks out.* **Father** *calls after him.*

Father   Gearóid.

Aunty Eily   Let him go, Jack.

Father (*after* **Gearóid**)   We're not forgetting the manifesto.

Boy   Strike a blow. Strike a blow.

Aunty Eily   He's nothing but a big, full-Irish bully.

Father   The country is unfinished. We have to stand firm.

Aunty Eily   Look. You're doing all the right things, Jack. You married the kindest woman in the world. You have a lovely German-Irish family. Don't let that man bully you. Don't let him talk you into bullying your own family. Come on, it's Christmas. Let's have a song. (*Beat.*) Now. Irmgard.

Silence. **Father** *sits down.* **Aunty Eily** *nods.* **Mother** *sings 'Wooden Heart' by Elvis Presley.*

Mother   Can't you see, I love you
Please don't break my heart in two . . .
. . . 'Cause I don't have a wooden heart.

Her voice breaks while she sings.

Aunty Eily   Irmgard.

Father   She's a bit homesick.

Stiegler *appears and steps up behind the* **Mother**, *putting on his jacket.*

Stiegler   Don't look so tragic, my dear. It's not the end of the world.

Beat.

Give me a smile.

Mother   No.

Stiegler   I brought you to the opera. Be a nice girl.

Mother   No.

Stiegler   You don't want anything to happen to your uncle, now do you?

Mother   No.

Stiegler   Come on. Big smile.

Mother *stands with an enforced smile on her face as the lights go down.*

End of Act Two.

Act Three

The stage is lit. The same minimal architecture with only one key addition. There is a beehive standing on stage.

We hear the buzzing music of Ligeti – 'Ramifications'.

Father *enters from the right dressed as a beekeeper and wearing beekeeper's mesh covering his head. On his arms he wears white, elbow-length gloves. He walks like an astronaut, limping across the stage with his arms in the air.*

The **Boy** *enters from the left, tracking the* **Father** *as he crosses the stage.*

Boy   Now is the time of the bees. And everybody is getting stung.

Father *kneels down on one knee with his hand on the top of the hive, facing towards the audience.*

Father   We'll show them. We'll show them that we have no weakness. No fear and no weakness and no history holding us back.

They said it was my limp. Something in the family. Big crowd outside the house. Standing in the street. Waiting for him to be brought out. They said I was not right in the head either because I had the limp from birth.

They didn't think I was going to be where I am today. With my own family. And my own bees. They're going to be afraid of us now. They're going to be afraid of us and there is nothing they can do to stop you flying out across the walls. (*Beat.*) Now.

Father *stands up and steps back to admire the hive. He removes the beekeeping mesh from his head. As he takes off the long white gloves he begins to look at the ceiling. He steps back further towards the centre of the stage, peering up at the ceiling from various angles.*

Father   Irmgard. Come and look at this.

Mother *enters from the left.*

Mother   What is it?

Father   Hanni, come here at once.

Boy *comes running forward.*

Boy   Yes.

Father   Did you do that?

Boy   What?

Father (*points up*)   The ceiling. Look at it.

Mother (*looks up*)   I don't believe it.

Father   We'll never get that off.

Mother   Have you gone out of your mind?

Boy   Yes.

Father   Did you do it?

Boy   No.

Father   I don't believe him.

Mother   Hanni, is that an Irish no?

Boy   Yes.

Mother   Yes?

Boy   No.

Mother   An Irish yes?

Boy   No.

Mother   A German no?

Boy   Yes.

Father (*angry*)   Who else would have done it?

Mother   Hanni, be honest. Did you throw the mashed potato at the ceiling?

Boy   No.

Mother   Is that a silent yes?

Boy   No.

Mother   The silent negative.

Boy   Yes.

Father (*barking*)   Answer the question. Yes or no?

Pause.

Boy   No.

Father   He's lying.

Mother   Hanni. You can never tell a lie. When somebody asks you a question, you must always tell the truth.

Boy   Yes.

Father   He's going to be punished for this.

Mother   Why did you do it?

Boy   For Ireland.

Father   The stick.

Mother   No wait. Seán. He said it was for Ireland.

Father   What?

Mother *places her hand on the* **Boy***'s shoulder.*

Mother   You must believe him.

Father   This is absurd.

Mother   It's artistic.

Father   Mashed potato.

Mother   That's the point. You have to have an imagination to do something that makes no sense. (*Beat.*) For your country.

Father (*pointing up*)   How is that going to help our country?

Mother   It's the principle, Seán.

Father   Is this what they do in Germany?

Mother   He's doing his best.

Father   Doing his worst, you mean.

Mother   Look. Sometimes he gets it wrong. But you can't punish him if he did it for Ireland.

Silence. **Father** *looks up at the ceiling, then down at the* **Boy**.

Father   Was it for Ireland?

Boy   Yes.

Father   Is that the truth?

Boy   Yes.

Father   The Irish truth?

Mother   The German truth?

Father   The only truth. And nothing but the truth?

Boy (*cheerfully*)   Yes.

Mother *and* **Father** *continue looking in rotation at the ceiling and at each other and at the* **Boy**. **Father** *puts his beekeeping mesh back on again and walks offstage.*

Mother   Only you could think of something as mad as that. Mashed potato on the ceiling. It's like something Franz Kaiser would have done. Your grandfather went into the bakery once and stuck his finger into a cake and lifted it up. How much is this? He asked. They told him the price.

She mimes holding up the cake on her index finger, then wipes it off.

Too expensive, he said and he put the cake back. But then he smiled and bought the cake after all. And he bought cakes for all the children on the Buttermarkt square as well. (*Beat.*) Mashed potato.

Mother *smiles at him and walks away to her writing desk.*

Boy My mother is good at rescuing us and making detours around my father. She tries to save us from the bees as well and beats them off with a kitchen towel. But sometimes it's too late and she can't stop herself from getting stung.

Stiegler *walks on to the stage left and picks up the* **Mother**'s *diary.* **Mother** *stands facing the audience.*

At night, the bees start buzzing around the light bulb. Buzzing and bouncing against the ceiling. Like an angry motorbike. Everybody is afraid. Everybody has their own nightmares of getting stung in the dark.

Stiegler *stands by the table leafing through the diary. He looks up.*

Stiegler What's this?

Mother My diary.

Stiegler Have you lost your senses?

Mother I have nobody else.

Stiegler This is evidence. You can't keep this.

Mother *looks helplessly at* **Stiegler**.

Mother I don't know what to do.

Stiegler Are you certain?

Mother Yes.

Stiegler Have you told anyone?

Mother No.

Stiegler Good.

Mother I'm afraid to speak.

Stiegler Now listen carefully to what I'm going to say. I want you to go back to your apartment, right now. Don't meet anyone. Don't speak to anyone. Go straight to your room and wait for me there. Do you understand what I've said?

Mother   Yes.

Mother *stands without moving. A moment in doubt.*

Stiegler   It will take me a while.

Mother   There is nobody else I can turn to.

Stiegler (*raising his voice*)   Well then.

Mother   What?

Stiegler (*shouting*)   I told you what to do. I'm not going to say it again. Go back to your place and wait. (*Pause.*) And don't speak to anyone. You hear.

Mother *stalls and watches* **Stiegler** *leafing through her diary.*

I'll dispose of this.

Stiegler *walks away with the diary.* **Mother** *walks over to the bed and sits down.*

Father *returns to the stage with a smoker – beekeeping apparatus. He puffs smoke into the air and then kneels down to puff smoke into the hive.*

Boy   My father has to make sure the bees won't escape. He talks to them in Irish, but the only thing that calms them down is smoke. It makes them drunk and happy and maybe they won't swarm away to a new place.

Bully Boys *pass across the front of the stage.* **Bully Boy 2** *has a ball under his arm and begins to limp around comically. The* **Boy** *watches.*

Bully Boy 1   Look at your man.

Bully Boy 2   The Irish beekeeper.

Bully Boy 1   Goebbels O'Hopalong.

Bully Boy 2   The Irish limp.

Bully Boy 1   One foot on and one foot off.

Bully Boy 2   Imagine him taking a penalty.

Bully Boy 2 *places the ball down and steps back. Then limps up to the ball and instead of kicking it he pretends that it's a rock.*

Bully Boy 2   Aagh. Jaysus.

Bully Boy 1 *laughs while* **Bully Boy 2** *limps around in a circle miming pain.*

Bully Boy 1   You spa.

Bully Boy 2   Limp. Hop. Limp. Hop. Limp. Hop.

Bully Boy 1   Sprecken the Gaelic.

Bully Boy 2 (*chanting*)   Tottenham Hotspurs.

Bully Boy 1 and 2 (*chanting*)   Tottenham Hotspurs. Tottenham Hotspurs. Tottenham Hotspurs. Tottenham Hotspurs.

Bully Boy 2   Come on Spurs.

The **Bully Boys** *exit, cheering. Silence.*

Boy   Tottenham Hotspurs. Tottenham Hotspurs. Tottenham Hotspurs.

Father *rips off his beekeeping hat and turns on the* **Boy**.

Father   What are you saying?

Boy   Nothing.

Father   You said something.

Boy   No.

Father   Yes you did. You were listening to them. Weren't you?

Father *begins to pull the* **Boy** *over to a chair. He furiously takes off the beekeeping gloves as the* **Mother** *comes forward.*

Mother   What's the matter?

Father   He was listening to them in English.

Mother   My God. This is going too far.

Father   I want him to be better than the boys going up to the football field.

Mother   No more punishment, please.

Father   I want him to learn, learn, learn. I want him to be meticulous. I want him to have more in his head than football.

Five times seven?

Boy   Thirty-two.

Father   Wrong.

Mother   What are you doing, Seán?

Father   I'm asking him a simple arithmetic question. Five multiplied by seven?

Mother   You can't use learning as punishment.

Father   That's how I got to where I am today, Irmgard.

Mother   Punishment?

Father   Education. (*To the* **Boy**.) Come on, think.

Father *begins marching up and down the stage with his limp.*

Boy (*thinking hard*)   Twenty-eight.

Father   You're guessing. Think again. Five by seven makes.

Boy (*making a face*)   Five times seven. Five by seven. Makes. Makes. Thirty-nine.

Father   He's not even trying.

Mother   Try a bit harder, Hanni.

Boy   Tottenham Hotspur.

Father (*stops walking*)   What?

Mother   He's trying to concentrate.

Father   Are you speaking English inside your head?

Boy   Spur.

Mother   This is no time for the silent negative, Hanni.

Father   He knows the right answer.

Mother   Hanni, please. Give him the right answer.

Boy   Hot.

Father   He's being stubborn.

Mother   Where did he pick that up?

Boy   I've got my father's anger and my mother's laughing.

Father   Speak up.

Boy   My father's winning and my mother's losing.

Mother   He's afraid to speak.

Boy   My father's history and my mother's history.

Father   He's only pretending.

Boy   My father's speeches and my mother's stories.

Mother   He's imagining something.

Father   This is the last time I'm going to ask you. Five by seven.

Pause.

Boy   Tottenham Hotspur.

Father   That's it.

*The **Father** strides over to the **Boy**, but the **Boy** runs away. The **Father** chases him around the stage.*

Boy   My father's voice and my mother's smile and father's fighting and my mother's courage and my father's shouting and my mother's crying.

Father   Come gummy here.

Boy   My mother's sadness and my father's madness.

Mother   Wait. Let me try in German.

Father   This is out of your hands, Irmgard.

Mother   Five times seven, Hanni?

The **Boy** *runs around the stage.* **Father** *tries to trap him.*

Boy   My mother's dreaming and my father's limping.

Mother   Just give in, Hanni. Please. For me.

Boy   Thirty-five.

Mother   Correct. He said it. Thirty-five.

Father   Too late.

Mother   Please Seán. I beg you. Think of Connemara.

Father   What?

Mother   Think of Connemara and all the stone walls.

Father   That's got nothing to do with this.

Mother   Think of the emptiness. Think of the wind. Remember the wind pushing us back on the strand.

Father *looks at the* **Boy** *again.*

Boy   Hotspur.

Father   You little gummy.

The **Father** *makes another lunge at the* **Boy**. **Boy** *flees across the stage with the* **Father** *in pursuit. The* **Boy** *is too fast and keeps getting away.* **Mother** *implores the* **Father** *to calm down as they continue running around the stage.*

Mother   Think of the bogs, Seán. The bogs and the wind and the water and nothing else in the world.

Father (*shouting*)   It's irrelevant.

Mother (*despairing*)   The water whispering.

Mother *stares into space. The* **Boy** *limps around the stage and the* **Father** *stops.*

Father   He's imitating me.

Boy   Hopalong.

Father   He's mocking me.

Mother   Hanni. Stop it.

Boy (*limping*)   Hop limp. Hop limp. Hop limp.

Father   He's no better than those boys out there.

Mother   Hanni. That's unforgivable.

Boy   Limp hop. Limp hop.

Father   Laughing at his own father.

Mother   Hanni. Stop it right now. You can never laugh at somebody else's weakness.

Father *calmly goes over to take a stick down from the top of the wardrobe. He lashes the stick against the side of the wardrobe with a whack.*

Father (*shouting*)   Come here.

Silence. The **Boy** *surrenders and goes over to the* **Father**.

Mother   Say you're sorry, Hanni.

Boy   I'm sorry.

Mother   He said he was sorry.

Father   Keep out of this, Irmgard.

Father *forces the* **Boy** *to kneel down, facing the audience.* **Father** *kneels down beside him and blesses himself. He places the cane on the floor.*

Father   In the name of the father and son and the holy ghost. (*Pause.*) We kneel here before you to pray at a most difficult time in our family.

Boy   We have to ask God what the punishment is going to be.

Father   Lord help us to fight this mockery and resistance.

Boy   God has to decide how many lashes.

Father   We ask you to be fair in your judgement.

Boy   Let me off, please.

Father   Twenty.

Boy   I'll pray every day.

Father   Minus five.

Boy   I promise with my hand on my heart that I will never laugh at my father's weakness again.

Father   Five lashes to be suspended.

Boy   Please.

Father   We thank you lord for making this (*beat*) difficult decision. In the name of the father and the son and the holy ghost. Amen.

Father *picks up the cane and pulls the* **Boy** *away offstage.*

Mother *pacing up and down at the centre of the stage.*

We hear the lash of the stick. Silence.

An air raid siren comes up – drowning out the lash of the stick.

Stiegler *enters, carrying a traditional, rounded doctor's leather case. He places the case on the chair by the writing desk. He opens the case and takes out some medical paraphernalia. Disinfectant. Cotton wool. Syringe. Rubber sheet. He places the rubber sheet on the bed.*

Stiegler   Lie down.

Mother *sits down on the bed.*

Mother   Is there going to be an injection?

Stiegler   This is the only way.

Mother   Where did you get it?

Stiegler   You don't need to know that.

Mother   What's in it?

Stiegler   Lie down.

Mother   What if it goes wrong?

Stiegler *leans down over her in a most threatening way.*

Stiegler   Now let's be very clear about this. You are aware of what we're doing here.

Mother   Yes.

Stiegler   We are about to commit a very serious crime.

Mother   I know that.

Stiegler   We are taking a baby away from the Führer.

Mother   But it's your baby.

Stiegler   It's Hitler's baby.

Mother   I can't have Hitler's baby.

Stiegler   Then you know what this means, don't you? We can never speak about it to anyone. Is that absolutely clear?

Mother *looks away.*

Now lie down. You have no other choice.

Mother *lies down.* **Stiegler** *pushes her dress up to expose her leg. He rubs alcohol on a spot at the upper thigh. He prepares the injection. He holds the syringe up in the air, stalls for a moment in this position, then turns towards the* **Mother** *to administer the injection.*

The **Boy** *runs back on to the stage to the front, left.*

Boy   I promise that the sting is NOT going to hurt. I promise that I am NOT who I am. I will NOT feel anything. I will NOT remember anything. I will NOT have any questions to ask.

Stiegler *begins to pack everything away into the doctor's bag.*

Stiegler   You must stay still and let things take their course.

He finishes packing up the bag and turns to her again.

You will thank me for this one day.

Stiegler *walks out. Sound of siren and bombing carries on for a moment, then begins to fade out.*

Silence.

Father *returns and puts the stick back on top of the wardrobe.*

Father   Are we friends again?

Boy   Yes.

Father   Come over here.

Boy *goes over to* **Father**. **Father** *puts his arm around him.*

Give me a smile.

Boy   I can't.

Father   You know that I love you.

Boy   Yes.

Father   You know that I want the best for you.

Boy   Yes.

Father   So come on. Give me a big smile.

Boy   I have no smile.

Father   Of course you have.

Boy   I lost it.

Father   No you haven't.

Father *puts his hand up to the* **Boy**'s *face. He prises the* **Boy**'s *lips apart and forces a smile, more like a grimace.*

There you are. Look. Big smile.

Boy *is left standing with an exaggerated grimace, frozen on his face.*

Sound of the siren and bombing returns. **Mother** *sits on the bed, holding her stomach.*

Mother   God help us.

Mother *gathers the rubber sheet around her and makes her way offstage. The siren and the bombing sounds hold for a moment, then subside.*

Father   It's all behind us now. Sit down. I'm going to teach you how to play chess.

Father *goes over and pulls up a chair and a small table. He begins to set up the chess game.* **Boy** *sits on the floor.*

Boy   Now it's the end of punishment. It's all over and forgotten. We're friends for life and we play chess every day and my father always wins.

Mother *appears on stage and takes the stick down from the wardrobe. She breaks the stick over her knee and then breaks the pieces again methodically, throwing them on the floor. She leaves again.*

My mother is looking for all the sticks in the house to make sure they can never be used against anyone again. She's going to break every stick in Ireland if she has to.

Mother *returns with a pile of sticks including a hurling stick.*

Otherwise there will be no end to it and the punishment will go on and on, lash by lash from the beginning of time all the way into the future. Because the people getting punished will always try and punish somebody else into infinity.

Mother *crosses the stage and leaves, carrying the pile of sticks with her.*

Now she's gone out to find a friend for us. Because we're too much in the house and we need good company.

Father   It's all about winning. It's all about finding the opponent's weakness. You can never show any mercy. You can never give in. And the most important thing of all to remember is this. You must shake hands after every game.

Mother *enters left and crosses the stage. The* **Shopkeeper** *enters right.* **Father** *and* **Boy** *continue studying the chessboard with great intensity.*

Mother   Missersmiss.

Shopkeeper   Misses O.

Mother   Missersmiss. I have an emergency. Could I ask you something?

Shopkeeper   By all means. Misses O.

Mother   My son. He needs a friend.

Shopkeeper   A friend?

Mother   He needs to get out. He needs to be in good company. Can you recommend anyone?

Shopkeeper   What about the doctor's son?

Mother   Does he speak Irish?

Shopkeeper (*beat*)   He's got red hair.

Mother   That will not be sufficient. He will have to undergo an examination.

Shopkeeper   Examination.

Mother   In the front room.

Shopkeeper   The front room. Ah, he wouldn't stand a chance.

Mother   Is he hopeless?

Shopkeeper   You could always tell your husband that he wants to learn Irish.

Mother   Yes. Of course. Now I know what you are saying. If he comes to our house he will soon be fluent. Then he'll go home and talk to his father in Irish. Then the doctor will talk to all his patients in Irish. And then the whole country will be speaking the language.

Shopkeeper   I wouldn't go that far.

Mother   It's a golden opportunity.

Shopkeeper   He'll go for the cakes at least.

Mother   Fair play to you.

Shopkeeper   No bother. Leave it to me, Misses O. I'll have a word.

Mother *walks away across the stage exiting.* **Shopkeeper** *looks on for a moment with a mystified expression.*

The front room.

Shopkeeper *shakes his head and leaves.*

Father   What?

Boy   Nothing.

Father   You want to ask me something?

Boy   No.

Father   Why don't you ask me?

Boy   What?

Father   How are you going to find out if you don't ask?

Boy   I don't know.

Father   What are you afraid of?

Boy   Things I don't want to hear.

Father   Look, son. I want you to have an enquiring mind. I want you to challenge the world and not be afraid to ask questions.

Boy   I don't know any questions.

Father   Anything that comes into your head.

Boy   Like who made the universe?

Father   God. That's obvious.

Boy   Who made God?

Father   That's not a question.

Mother *re-enters left and watches the chess game from a distance.*

Boy   What year was the battle of Clontarf?

Father   You should know that.

Boy   Seven times thirteen.

Father   Don't start acting the schoolteacher.

Boy   Who is Winston Churchill?

Father   Are you trying to provoke me?

Mother *begins to speak as though she's whispering in the* **Boy**'s *ear.*

Mother   Ask him about his father.

Boy   Why did you lock the sailor in the wardrobe?

Father (*beat*)   That's none of your business.

Mother   Ask him about the First World War.

Boy   Did they fight against each other?

Father   Who?

Boy   My Irish grandfather and my German grandfather.

Father   Not face to face.

Boy   But they were enemies?

Father   Your grandfather John Hamilton fought for the British and that's why we don't talk about him in this house with a German mother.

Mother   Ask him what happened.

Boy   How did the sailor die?

Father   That's got nothing to do with you.

Boy   Who killed him?

Father   What?

Boy   Was it Michael Collins?

Father   Nobody killed him. For God's sake. (*Beat.*) Look. You're not going to use this against me?

Boy   No.

Father   He died. (*Beat.*) In a mental hospital.

Boy   Why?

Father   He tried to kill me.

Boy   How?

Father   With a knife.

Boy   When?

Father   You're not going to tell anyone about this, are you?

Boy   No.

Father   None of your friends?

Boy   Which friends?

Father   He fell on board a battleship in a storm. From one deck down on to a lower deck. He hit his head.

Beat.

He started losing his memory and they sent him home. Discharged. Incoherent. He just sat by the window all day trying to remember something that was gone out of his head. One day he picked up a knife in the kitchen. He pointed the knife at me. He said he was going to kill me if I didn't stop asking him questions.

Pause.

My mother had to stand in the way. You'll have to kill me first, she said.

Pause.

Then he was taken away. Up to the mental hospital in Cork. Everybody was out on the street when the men came for him in a car. She was crying. My mother. She said he would be back soon. Before long. But he never came back.

We went up on the train to visit him. He was lying on the bed in his room. My mother spoke his name. But he turned away to face the wall.

Boy   Was he homesick?

Father   He didn't want to talk to me.

Boy   Is that why you turned against him?

Father   He didn't recognise his own son.

Boy   What did you do with his uniform?

Father   Why do you want to know all this?

Boy   I'm trying to find your weakness.

Father   I have no weakness.

Boy   Yes you do.

Father   What?

Boy   It's checkmate.

Father   No it's not.

Boy   You have nowhere to go.

Father   Wait.

Father *stares down at the chessboard.*

Boy   You have to shake hands.

Boy *stands up and stretches out his hand.* **Father** *stares up at the boy.*

Father   Wait till I make my move.

Father *suddenly looks at the audience. Then he looks back at the boy. Finally he looks at the chessboard once more and flips the table with the chess game up in the air. He stands up and storms offstage, right.* **Boy** *is left there with the chess pieces rolling around his feet.*

Mother *goes to the* **Boy** *and speaks directly to him.*

Mother   Leave it. We're not picking this up.

Boy   I hate him. He's not my father.

Mother   No Hanni. If you hate your father then you'll hate yourself.

Boy   I want to run away and never come back.

Mother *kneels down and takes the* **Boy**'s *hands in hers.*

Mother   Hanni. You have to understand your father's nightmare.

Boy   He didn't shake hands.

Mother   You are the adult now and he is the child.

Boy   I'm going down to the sea to kill the bully waves.

Boy *breaks away from her.*

Mother   Don't pass on the punishment, Hanni. No more sticks. No more stones.

Boy   I'm going to live under the waves and never come up for words.

Mother   Be big-hearted.

Boy   I'll never speak again. EVER.

Boy *runs away offstage.* **Mother** *calls after him.*

Mother   But I've found a friend for you. (*Beat.*) The doctor's son.

We hear the waves crashing. Dog barking. **Boy** *re-enters and runs to the front of the stage, picking up stones and throwing them.*

Boy   I hate the waves. I hate the dog with no name. You're not my friend. You belong to nobody and you're no good to anyone. Nobody wants you. They won't even miss you when you're gone. Get down under the bully waves until your lungs burst. Get down. Get down. Get down and never come up.

Throwing stones with great urgency. Barking stops.

Jaysus what the Jaysus.

Boy *stands for a moment in silence. He looks left and right, then runs away offstage left.*

Bully Boy 1 *enters right, followed by* **Bully Boy 2**.

Bully Boy 1   Did you see that? I swear. He's after drowning the dog.

Bully Boy 2   Nazi murderer.

Bully Boy 1   Drowned the dog with no name.

Bully Boy 2   Senseless killing. That is genocide.

Bully Boy 1   Don't be stupid. That's for people.

Bully Boy 2   He killed an innocent dog. That's inhuman.

Bully Boy 1   After him.

Bully Boy 2   No mercy.

Bully Boy 1   You have nowhere to hide.

Bully Boy 2   Nowhere.

They run away offstage left.

Gearóid *enters from the right with a newspaper in his hand.*

Gearóid   Ah. The woman of the house.

Mother   He's still at work.

Gearóid   Still keeping the people of Mullingar in the dark.

Mother   We are all in the dark now.

Gearóid   How are the bees doing?

Mother   They are everywhere, all over the house.

Gearóid   Multiplying and gathering as we speak. (*Beat.*) If only we could out-populate our enemies.

Mother   With children, you mean?

Gearóid   The children are the best weapon we have.

Mother   Will you go away.

Gearóid   They are the foot soldiers. The front line.

Mother   You must be joking. That's what Hitler said.

Gearóid   Your husband is a true beekeeper.

Mother   We are not bees.

Gearóid   A great idealist.

Mother   I would prefer him to be a great father.

Gearóid   He was my right-hand man. Loyal party member to the very end. Long after the others defected. He gave great speeches. Outside the GPO. Had the crowd in the palm of his hand.

Mother   He has the family in the palm of his hand.

Gearóid   He spoke with great vision.

Mother   It is hard to stop a man with a vision.

Gearóid   Powerful speeches about the Jews.

Mother   The Jews?

Gearóid   During the war years. He wrote a great piece for our newspaper. Aiseirí. Which they tried to censor. But we published it. Because it was so well written. And very fair-minded.

Mother   What did he say?

Gearóid   All about the Jews exploiting the Irish people. How the Jews would have to conform and be Irish like everyone else. And play hurling. And do Irish dancing.

Mother   Irish dancing?

Gearóid   Brilliant piece. Did you never read it?

Mother   No I didn't.

Gearóid   Maybe he didn't go far enough.

Gearóid *places the newspaper on the small table.*

The latest edition. Straight off the press.

He turns away.

Will you tell him I dropped in. (*Beat.*) I'll be back.

Gearóid *leaves.*

The **Boy** *enters at the front of the stage right.*

Mother *turns and looks at the wardrobe. She goes to the wardrobe and opens the doors wide. Then she begins to search, taking out all kinds of documents and throwing them on the floor.*

Boy   All the letters and the train tickets. All the restaurant receipts and the hotel bills from the honeymoon. All the napkins with the coffee stains. All the souvenirs and the postcards of the Rhine. Tickets for the opera and tickets for the cable car up the Drachenfels.

Mother *continues taking items out of the wardrobe. A picture of the sailor is revealed at the back of the wardrobe. She finally comes across a newspaper and begins to read.* **Father** *walks in and drops his briefcase with a clack. He takes off his cap.*

Father   Irmgard.

Father *limps across the stage and stops, looking at the* **Mother** *kneeling on the floor with all his personal items spread around.* **Mother** *holds up the newspaper.*

Mother   You kept this from me.

Father   You have no right to look at my things.

Mother   You never said a word.

Father   I don't read your personal diaries.

Mother   This is public.

Father   It's a long time ago.

Mother   My sister saved the life of a Jewish woman.

Father   Things were different back then.

Mother   Without the help of Marianne, she would have been taken away and (*beat*) and murdered.

Father   We were neutral.

Mother   Marianne took her into her house. On the mountain. After the war, the woman was able to start a new life in America.

Mother *drops the newspaper from her hand and gets up from the floor.*

Father   I'm sure there are things you haven't told me.

Mother   You refuse to admit it.

Father   It's all in the past, Irmgard.

Mother   It's the hardest thing, isn't it?

Father   What?

Mother   You can't say you were wrong.

Father   Am I wrong because I didn't know any better?

The **Mother** *looks at him without moving.*

Am I wrong because I wanted to do something for my country? Because I tried to achieve something? Because I believed in something that could not be achieved?

Mother *turns and walks away. He continues shouting after her.*

Am I wrong because I didn't win? Because everyone was against me? Because the language is dying?

Pause.

Am I wrong because I have a limp?

*The **Father** goes to get his beekeeping gear from behind the armchair and begins to put it on. He puts on his working coat and buttons up. He puts the headgear on and then the long, white elbow-length gloves.*

Boy   I'm afraid to go home. I'm afraid of the full silence.

Beat.

I want them to be friends again. Like they were on holidays in Connemara. When everything was still in the future. With no footprints yet. When my father was happy and my mother said it was like walking on the moon. When we sheltered in a doorway and my father had his arm around her. When we were dreaming and staring at the rain falling and listening to the water whispering along the side of the road like the only language allowed.

*The **Boy** stands frozen at the front of the stage as the **Bully Boys** appear.*

Bully Boy 1   Hey Hitler.

Bully Boy 2   We saw you drowning the dog.

Bully Boy 1   You're guilty.

Boy   I've been executed before already.

Bully Boy 1   Don't get smart, Hitler. Why did you kill the dog?

Boy   He was not my friend.

Bully Boy 1   You shall be executed.

Silence.

Bully Boy 2 (*screaming*)   Larry Eichmann.

Silence.

Bully Boy 1   Death penalty.

Bully Boys *suddenly rush to execute him. Each thump of their fists accompanying a word.*

Bully Boy 2   Swastika.

Bully Boy 1   Hund.

Bully Boy 2   Blitzen.

Bully Boy 1   Schwein.

Bully Boy 2   Blitzen.

The **Boy** *fights back, flailing his arms and shouting in a frenzy.*

Boy   Jaysus what the Jaysus. Blitzen Jaysus Blitzen. Larry Eichmann of an SS killer man with no mercy.

Bully Boys *retreat.*

Yes. Yes. Guilty for all the people in the freezing homesick of a Jewish place that belongs to nobody with suitcases in a heap of dead bodies and dead eyes shouting and Jaysus gas camps and what the Jaysus chimneys with all the people smoke and bones and crying, burning, crying, burning, burning, burning.

Bully Boy 1   Jaysus.

Bully Boy 2   Hitler is gone mental.

Bully Boy 1   He's out of his mind.

Bully Boy 2   Come on.

Bully Boys *run away.* **Boy** *stands for a moment and rubs his eyes with his sleeve.*

Boy   My weakness is going to make me strong.

Boy *walks away offstage right.*

The buzzing of Ligeti music rises once more. **Father** *steps towards the beehive at the centre of the stage and keels down on one knee to talk to them.*

Father   They've all turned against me now. Even my own son. You see the way he won't even talk to me any more. You see the way he ignores me in the street. There I was buying a newspaper and he came right up beside me. Hid away in a doorway when he heard my voice. Didn't want to know me. Watched me walking away towards the train station as though he had never seen me before in his life.

He lifts the lid off the hive.

Why does this happen to me?

The buzzing Ligeti music suddenly increases, exploding around the stage. A shadow leaps up from the hive, like a black cat jumping. The **Father** *fights off the bees and stumbles backwards. He is outraged at this revolt.*

Father (*shouts*)   No. No. No.

The **Father** *beats off the bees.*

Irmgard.

He tries to put the lid back on to the hive, but he fails to do so and continues beating off the bees.

No.

The **Mother** *runs on to the stage with a towel but is beaten back by the bees.*

Mother   More smoke.

Father *picks up the smoker and puffs at the bees.*

Father   It's no good.

Mother   Leave it.

Father   They've gone wild.

Mother   Get the lid back on.

The **Mother** *runs offstage for a moment. She reappears quickly, wearing a number of towels around her head for protection.*

Father   My mouth.

Father *stumbles back. He punches repeatedly at his own neck, trying to remain stoical, with an attitude of great hurt and indignation.*

Mother   Stand back.

The **Father** *stumbles forward towards her, dropping the smoker with a clack. She retreats from him, beating off the bees.* **Father** *beats himself again and again, all over his body. Mostly around the neck and the head.*

Father   Inside my ear.

Mother   Get away from the hive.

The **Father** *knocks off the headgear in desperation. The sound of buzzing music gets even louder. He slaps his own face and limps away across the stage. Then he stumbles forward once more and collapses on the floor, near the front of the stage. Buzzing music dies down a little.*

The **Mother** *is finally able to reach him and kneels down beside him. She beats the bees off him with a towel. Buzzing fades away as she begins to take bee stings out from his neck and face.*

Mother   How many stings have you got? One, two, three.

Father   I was wrong, Irmgard.

Mother   Five, six, seven, eight.

Father   I'm sorry.

Mother   Ten, twelve, thirteen.

Father   Aunty Eily was right.

Mother   Hold still.

Father   I turned my family into strangers.

Mother   Twenty-two. Twenty-three.

Father   I turned my back on my own father.

Mother   Twenty-eight.

Father   I'm sorry I made things so hard for you.

Mother   Thirty-two stings. My God. Stand up, Seán.

She makes him stand up, but he only manages to sit down on the bed.

Father   I made mistakes.

Mother   Come on. We better get you to the hospital.

Father   No, no. I made the wrong mistakes.

Mother   How do you know they're wrong until you make them?

Father   I never learned how to be a father. It's not something that was passed on to me.

Mother   There's still time. We need to hurry.

Mother *picks up his glasses from the floor and gives them to him. He puts them on and she tries to get him up, but he stalls again.*

Father   If I had my life over again, I would not make the same mistakes. I would make different mistakes.

Mother   Not the ones already made, you mean.

Father (*smiles*)   Other mistakes.

Mother   Better mistakes.

Father   The right mistakes.

Mother   You'll get the hang of it in the end.

Father   As long as you keep correcting me.

Mother   Here. Put your arm around me.

He puts his arm around her and they stand up. As they move away towards the right, he stops once more.

Father   Irmgard.

Beat.

You are the only mistake I didn't make.

Mother   Let's get you to the hospital.

She helps him off the stage.

*The **Boy** runs on to the stage and sees the destruction everywhere. Documents on the floor. The chess set upturned. The beehive left open. The bee protection mesh lying beside it.*

Boy *picks up the beekeeping mesh from the floor and holds it in his hands for a moment. Then he carefully places it away.*

Boy   The front door of the house has been left open now and the leaves are blowing in. Everybody can walk in off the street and look around the rooms at all our secrets.

We hear Elisabeth Schwarzkopf once more singing 'Der Freischutz'.

*The **Mother** returns to the stage and puts her arm around the **Boy**. **Aunty Eily** appears and embraces the **Mother**. Then she embraces the **Boy**. The **Shopkeeper** appears and shakes hands with the **Mother**, then with the **Boy**. **Gearóid** appears and shakes hands with the **Mother** and the **Boy**. He then also shakes hands with **Aunty Eily** and the **Shopkeeper**. The **Bully Boys** appear and everyone shakes hands all around. Finally, the **Bully Boys** shake hands with the **Boy**.*

Mother *goes to sit down on a chair at the table, facing the audience. The **Boy** goes to stand beside her and she takes his hands in hers. The others remain standing in a cluster upstage.*

Mother   Hanni. Your father made life very hard for himself. He did things that were wrong but there is something I want to tell you about him. When we were on our honeymoon, going down along the Rhine together on the train, he didn't talk very much. He was very shy. He waited for me to give him the first kiss. On the night of the honeymoon, I cried my first tears because I thought it was going to be a marriage without children. I waited and waited in the dark and didn't let him know I was crying. But then we managed to bring you back from the honeymoon with us after all. (*Beat.*) I carried you over to Ireland on the mail boat.

She pats her stomach.

In here.

*The **Boy** puts his arms around the **Mother** in a warm embrace.*

Hanni.

Boy   What?

Mother   You're cracking my bones.

Boy *lets go of the* **Mother**. *She smiles at him and stands up. She takes the **Boy**'s hand and leads him to the front of the stage.*

Let's go for a walk.

Aunty Eily, **Gearóid**, **Shopkeeper** *and the* **Bully Boys** *leave in different directions, moving away to the back and offstage. The sound of the foghorn is heard.*

Boy   Up the pier.

Mother   Up to the lighthouse.

Boy   With the finger pointing.

Mother   Round and round.

Boy   Across the water.

Mother   Listen.

*We hear the sound of the foghorn more clearly. Flash of the lighthouse crossing their faces at intervals. The **Boy** imitates the sound of the foghorn.*

Boy Room.

Mother Room.

Boy Room the room.

Mother Do you hear the echo?

The foghorn continues to sound intervals.

Boy Room the room.

Mother Try again.

Boy Hey. Out there.

Mother (*laughs*) Hey. Out there.

Boy Let's see how long the echo takes to come back. (*Shouting.*) We're over here in Ireland.

Mother One – two – three.

Boy We're over here in Ireland.

Mother We come from the town of Kempen.

Boy (*pause*) We come from the town of Kempen.

Mother Try it in Irish as well.

Boy But they don't like Irish.

Mother Of course they do. Ask them how they're getting on.

Boy How are you all over there and how did you know our language?

Mother (*laughs*) The question answering a question.

Boy How are you all getting on with the language over there?

Mother It's like laughing in the mirror. (*Beat.*) You know, maybe it doesn't matter what country you come from any more.

Boy Maybe your home is not a place.

Mother Maybe it's only a story that you make up in your head. A story full of all the things you remember and all the people you've met. All the beautiful things you've seen. All the mistakes and all the funny things.

The **Boy** *holds up his hand.*

Boy   Listen.

Faint sound of the dog barking.

Do you hear that?

Mother   What?

Boy   There.

They listen. The dog is heard barking again.

Mother   Yes. I hear it.

Boy (*elated*)   Barking.

Mother   Even a dog has an echo.

Boy   It's him.

Mother   Who?

Boy   The dog. The dog that belongs to nobody. He's alive.

Mother   He's barking isn't he?

Boy   He didn't drown. He's not dead. (*Beat.*) So I'm not a Nazi.

Mother   You never were a Nazi.

Mother *pats the* **Boy** *on the head.*

Don't get your shoes wet.

She walks away and leaves the **Boy** *alone facing the audience.*

Boy   When you're small you know nothing. You don't know who you are or where you are or what questions to ask.

Boy *puts his hands in his pockets.*

A **Sailor** *appears on the stage right. The same actor who played the father is now dressed in a British navy uniform of 1916. He* *walks on to the stage with no limp. Sound of waves unfolding on the shore. The* **Sailor** *picks up a stone and throws it at the waves. Dog barking.*

Boy   He's trying to hold back the waves.

Sailor   He won't get far with that.

Boy   I saw you in the wardrobe.

Sailor   You're the German-Irish boy.

Boy   Half and half.

Sailor   You have your hands in both pockets.

Boy   Speckled.

Beat.

Sailor   What language do you dream in?

Boy   We dream in Irish.

Sailor   And you wake up in German.

Boy   We cry in German.

Sailor   But you laugh in English.

Boy   We remember in Irish.

Sailor   You think ahead in German.

Boy   And we sing in English.

Pause.

Sailor   More homesick than seasick.

Pause. Foghorn.

Boy   More homesick than seasick.

The foghorn continues. Dog barking. Foghorn and barking more distant. Subsiding. Lights fade.

End of Act Three.

Printed in the USA
CPSIA information can be obtained
at www.ICGtesting.com
LVHW020900171024
794056LV00002B/646

9 781408 171189